THE

Short .... *...ctions*

Canon M. T. Coombe
(Canon of the Diocese of Gibraltar in Europe)

ARTHUR H. STOCKWELL LTD.
Torrs Park   Ilfracombe   Devon
Established 1898
www.ahstockwell.co.uk

British Library Cataloguing-in-Publication Data.
A catalogue record for this book is available
from the British Library.

ISBN 0 7223 3649-7
Printed in Great Britain by
Arthur H. Stockwell Ltd.
Torrs Park   Ilfracombe
Devon

Introduction

"The Lord said unto me, Amos, what seest thou? And I said, A plumb line. Then the Lord said, Behold, I will set a plumb line in the midst of my people Israel: I will not again pass by them any more"
(Amos 7 v8)

The prophet Amos lived in a time of great prosperity. He foresaw the dangers of such a situation for the Nation's spititual health. In one of his prophecies he sees the Lord standing beside a wall holding a plumb line. Amos' eye is on the plumb line, not the Lord, because he sees that the wall, God's Israel, is not straight and will soon fall. God's patience with the Nation is at an end.

As we think about our Lent, we see a parallel with our own times when so many seem to ignore religion and are self-complacent. Amos foresaw a rude awakening. Will we avoid one if we can bring about a spiritual revival in our own country? It is surely long overdue.

"They will sell the needy for a pair of shoes", Amos says.

Shriving Tuesday — Shrove Tuesday

Quote:
"Beware that thou forget not the Lord thy God in not keeping his commandments and his judgments and his statutes"
(Deuteronomy 8 v11)

Pancake day. In the Middle Ages the pancake played a large part at the beginning of Lent. A feast was held as the worst of the winter was over — a feast the day before Lent began and the day when sins were forgiven. It was the last chance for a holiday before the forty days of Lent. All eggs, butter or other fats were to be eaten. Rich foods and meat were to be given up. As it was a holiday games were played. Some continue now. Pancake races have been restored, probably the best known is at Olney. Abroad famous carnivals are held, in particular Mardi Gras in New Orleans. Shrove Tuesday held an important part in Christian lives. I hope it does for you as you go happily to your shriving.

Prayer:
"Lord we know that the earth is Yours and all that is in it, so let us rejoice and give thanks"

Ash Wednesday

Quote:
> *"Lay not up for yourselves treasures upon earth...*
> *but lay up for yourselves treasures in heaven"*
> *(Matthew 6 vv19-20)*

Lent begins. The word is simple and is derived from an Anglo-Saxon one meaning "springtime". We have kept the word in "Lengthen", as the days get longer, so it has no religious significance of its own. Just before this period, our Parish Priest asked for last year's palm crosses so that he could burn them and make ash to mark our foreheads as a penitential reminder of this time.

Many may give something up. A lady I know who loves her chocolate will do without it during Lent and contribute towards charity instead, but she still looks forward to restarting at Easter. Why not? Many will take on some extra duty. It is a personal choice and needs thought. Whatever you may do, make sure it is not gloomy. It is the Christian hope we are looking towards, nothing sad about that.

Prayer:
> *"We pray that our Lent may be a time of prayer,*
> *acceptable unto God"*

Thursday after Ash Wednesday

Quote:

"Rend your heart and not your garments"
(Joel 2 v13)

In some Churches there is a custom of removing or veiling crosses and statues and the clergy will be wearing purple or violet vestments. This development could be thought of as a misunderstanding of the old customs at the beginning of the Christian era. What was being veiled in these early days was not the cross but the splendour of rich metalwork. To obscure the cross especially later in Holy Week seems very misplaced and so we have the unveiling on Good Friday. Many Churches nowadays substitute a plain wooden cross with no figure on it for the more impressive ones that may be there.

Prayer:
"Be with us today, O Lord, as we begin our Christian warfare"

Friday after Ash Wednesday

Quote:

> *"Blow the trumpet in Zion, sanctify a fast"*
> *(Joel 2 v15)*

Lent is intended to be a time of spiritual renewal, a springtime for ourselves. Therefore it would be helpful to look at what Jesus was doing during the forty days. It was not just a period of fasting. The Gospel record which is a very sacred one indeed, as it can only have come from Him, suggests that He was talking with God the Father about how He was going to carry out the task God had laid upon Him. The temptations came towards the end of the period in the wilderness.

Prayer:

> *"We pray Lord that ours may be both a giving Lent*
> *and a giving-up Lent"*

Saturday after Ash Wednesday

Quote:
"Fear not, O land, for the Lord will do great things"
(Joel 2 v21)

Nothing is more deadly than a sham religion and nothing more easy for the Christian. Lent can, if we are not careful, degenerate into merely attending more services, saying more prayers, reading more books or of the Bible. There is nothing wrong in any of these things. It is the way we set about doing them and the spirit in which we undertake them that matters.

Prayer:
"We pray, Lord, for the help we need to carry out our Lenten resolutions. Give us strength to make them worthwhile"

First Sunday of Lent

Quote:

"Thou shalt worship the Lord thy God,
and him only shalt thou serve"
(Matthew 4 v10)

Past ages were noisy ones, ours is even more so, but where our Lord went for the temptations must have been utter silence, stillness and loneliness, very difficult for us to imagine. Try sitting still for a moment and you will soon realise how noisy we are, both inwardly in our minds and with external sounds. It is not enough to think as we are likely to of the peaceful English countryside. We have to think of rocky barren desolation until the Jews made recent changes. In Jesus' time we would have commented on the utter eeriness and absence of any sound by day or night. This is the background to the temptation story which we will look at this coming week.

Prayer:

"We pray today that we may be able to cultivate silence
in our lives at our prayer-time"

Monday in the second week of Lent

Quote:
"Then was Jesus led up of the spirit into the wilderness"
(Matthew 4 v1)

There are two general points about the temptation story which we should think about. The first has been touched on last week, namely the holiness of this time. It is really an inner spiritual biography of our Lord, and secondly how aware Jesus must have been of His quite exceptional powers to have had temptations, trials, tests, whatever we may call them, of this kind. It is after all no trouble to us to be tempted to turn pebbles into bread. As we know our trials are of a very different kind.

Prayer:
"Lord we pray that we may join in the sacredness of this time in the wilderness"

Tuesday in the second week of Lent

Quote:
"When Jesus had fasted forty days and forty nights,
he was afterward an hungered"
(Matthew 4 v2)

When we first heard the account of the temptations in the wilderness, we may have wondered what relevance they have to our lives. We would have been wrong if we thought there was no parallel to us at home or at work. Jesus is being asked by the Devil to take the easy way out of being very hungry. He could take the quick and easy way out of a problem. Should we stop at this point and ask ourselves if this ever happens to us. We probably say that it will only be this once!

Prayer:
"Lord give us the strength to withstand the desire to
take the wrong way out of our difficulties"

Wednesday in the second week of Lent

Quote:

> *"Then the devil taketh Jesus and setteth him*
> *on a pinnacle of the temple"*
> *(Matthew 4 v5)*

When Jesus was tempted to throw Himself off the top of the Temple, it was being suggested that He try something sensational to attract people. It would be headline news as we say nowadays and would be performed in front of a large crowd. There was always a large crowd at the Jerusalem Temple of people visiting from all over the then known world and it was not long since Herod the Great had completed the rebuilding. It was too the centre of religious life and administration for the Jews and would be much easier than long wearisome days teaching in Galilee. Sensation was the answer and would last as long as one — a few weeks perhaps. Peoples' memories are not long for the sensational. It would only have been a seven days' wonder.

Prayer:

> *"Lord help us to build Your Kingdom here on earth"*

Thursday in the second week of Lent

Quote:

> *"All these things will I give thee if thou wilt*
> *fall down and worship me"*
> *(Matthew 4 v9)*

Jesus was being asked to make a bargain. He could have all the riches of the world if He would worship Satan. He could be greater than Napoleon or Hitler or Stalin or Alexander the Great. We in our turn are offered bargains for the fulfilment of our desires for success, riches, prosperity, popularity or pleasure. Jesus was quite certain as we must be that we can never defeat evil by compromising with evil. Our Christianity cannot stoop to compromise. We have to raise ourselves to the level of Christ.

Prayer:

> *"Lord give us the strength we need to*
> *withstand our temptations"*

Friday in the second week of Lent

Quote:
"Then the devil leaveth him and angels came
and ministered unto him"
(Matthew 4 v11)

Our Lord's temptations and ours have then an underlying likeness and this should help us in our progress through Lent. Centuries ago Lent was the time when candidates for baptism underwent the last stages of their preparation. On Easter eve at their baptism they would turn to the setting sun and confess their sins and then turn east and profess their faith. It is right that we should be looking at ourselves at this time.

Prayer:
"May we find repentance and forgiveness in the blessing
of Christ's time in the wilderness"

Saturday in the second week of Lent

Quote:

"Hear my prayer, O Lord, and let my cry come unto thee"
(Psalm 102 v1)

We can picture Jesus alone in the wilderness and we know from the Gospel accounts what thoughts came to Him there and how He dealt with them. God's way for Him was to be the way of the cross, suffering and perfect love. At Gethsemane Satan would come again, but after the forty days the issue was resolved for the time being. Our Lord accepted the situation and Angels came to look after Him.

Prayer:

"Let us continue to pray for a happy and helpful Lent which finds us ready for the joyful feast of Easter"

Second Sunday of Lent

Quote:
"Keep us outwardly in our bodies and inwardly in our souls"
(From the Prayer Book Collect for today)

Today's Gospel reading in the Prayer Book is the story of Our Lord's visit to the area of Tyre and Sidon and His meeting with the clever repartee of the Canaanite woman. This is the only description of an occasion when Jesus is seen outside Jewish territory. So this passage foreshadows the going out of the Gospel to the whole world. Our Lord was looking for some privacy where He could talk to the disciples about the coming days of the cross. This is not Our Lord running away. He is preparing Himself and the disciples for the decisive battle to come.

Prayer:
"We pray that we too may share the faith of the woman in today's Gospel, so that we too may receive Our Lord's blessing"

Monday in the third week of Lent

Quote:
> *"And his disciples came and besought him, saying,*
> *Send her away"*
> *(Matthew 15 v23)*

This week with the above introductory quote, we are looking at various important words which appear in the New Testament. Today we look at the word "Disciples" who were first called Christians in Antioch. Disciples are learners, not advanced scholars, simple learners in the faith as we all are. We are all conscious of our ignorance and inability to answer questions which our friends ask us. We must always be willing to learn from our reading and prayers. This is how we all must begin.

Prayer:
> *"We pray that we may be given insight into our faith so*
> *that we can help others in their pilgrimage"*

Tuesday in the third week of Lent

Quote:
"More than ever believers were added to the Lord,
multitudes both of men and women"
(Acts 5 v14)

The word "Disciple" drops out of use after the Gospels for Christians are people of faith, so from an early date the word "believer" is used, as in our quote. Christians were identified by their faith. Faith is primarily committal, not just believing in a creed, but trusting, so St Paul says "If you believe in your heart that God raised Jesus from the dead, you will be saved". The early Church was very effective, crowds joined them. We need to recover this faith.

Prayer:
"Lord increase our faith, that we may speak effectively to others"

Wednesday in the third week of Lent

Quote:
"To all God's believers in Rome, who are called saints"
(Romans 1 v7)

"Saints" is one of the commonest words used for Christians in the New Testament. We need to look at the word carefully because its meaning has changed. To us it means eminent Christians or a very holy or virtuous person who has been marked out by his or her Church and canonised. To many non-Christians they may be rather artificially associated with stained glass windows. To the early Church Christians were all Saints. It meant someone dedicated to God in Christ, a forgiven sinner, our aim this Lent.

Prayer:
"We give thanks for all our Christian brethren and the example they give us to follow"

Thursday in the third week of Lent

Quote:
"Go to my brethren and tell them that I am ascending to
my Father, My God and your God"
(John 20 v17)

Jesus was the first to call His followers "'Brothers". It is
therefore a very important title and no wonder the early
Church adopted it so willingly. It means that we all,
brothers and sisters have entered on a very vital spiritual
relationship with God, something we are exploring in
great hope this Lent. We are members then of an
enormous group, not Christians in isolation which some
would like to be. We all differ, but in spite of our
differences we are aware of the bond which unites us
as the family of God here on earth. But it is not enough
merely to recognise this, we have to demonstrate it and
love our fellow Christians accordingly.

Prayer:
"We pray that our love for each other may grow
stronger as we try to show it"

Friday in the third week of Lent

Quote:

"I beseech you as strangers and pilgrims"
(1 Peter 2 v11)

Today's word "Pilgrim" is less familiar than some we have looked at this week. Probably we would first remember John Bunyan and his book *"Pilgrim's Progress"*, written in Bedford Gaol and not so often read nowadays. It is nevertheless a thoroughly biblical theme founded on both Testaments. For Scripture is a view of the Christian life as a pilgrimage. In our earthly pilgrimage we are challenged to live and work for our Lord in our daily lives and business. To the early Christian pilgrims, heaven was very real and they talked and sang a great deal about it. We too must look forward in hope.

Prayer:
"We pray that we may offer ourselves for our fellow pilgrims and seek to help them"

Saturday of the third week in Lent

Quote:

"To the servants of Christ Jesus"
(Philippians 1 v1)

In what sense are we "Servants" in this list of words we have been looking at this week." Servant" is not a word we use nowadays, but Our Lord does command us to do what He says in particular the command He gives us at the first Maundy Thursday supper — that we should take bread and wine in remembrance of Him — how does this life of service work for us? The Lord has work for each one of us to do, a vocation to follow or a ministry to fulfil. Living a Christian life is not a kind of luxury cruise, it is for rendering service that the world looks to the Church today.

Prayer:
"Pray that we may be shown what work is to be done today"

Third Sunday of Lent

Quote:
*"Stretch forth the right hand of thy Majesty, to be
our defence against all our enemies"
(from the collect for 3rd Sunday in Lent)*

The Jewish authorities were by now very concerned about the effect Jesus' ministry was having on the ordinary folk of Galilee and the likely possibility of rebellion against the Roman occupying power, so they resorted to slander. They declared that His powers came from the Devil. Jesus gave them a double and crushing answer. He pointed out that many Jews cast out devils so they too must be in league with Satan. He also says that if the devils are being removed by their own leader, then his kingdom will not last long. He is finished. Therefore if I cast out devils, I must be stronger than him by your own argument.

Prayer:
*"Lord, Your word is life for us — may we read
and study Your words carefully"*

Monday in the fourth week of Lent

Quote:

"When Jesus was come near, he beheld
the city, and wept over it"
(Luke 19 v41)

Our Lord made many visits to the capital city, but none so overwhelming as the one from which today's quote comes and our thoughts this week. He foresaw that the chaotic state of Judaism could only lead to its collapse and the enormity of the tragedy which would engulf His people. This hurt the really human Jesus to the full. We do well to think about Our Lord's humanity at all times.

Prayer:

"We pray that we may help in the doing of
God's work in the world"

Tuesday in the fourth week of Lent

Quote:

> *"Be ye therefore followers of God as dear children"*
> *(Ephesians 5 v1)*

The old prophets picture the people of Israel going to Jerusalem for instruction in God's ways and so re-establish the divine order which God intended for the world at its creation. But Jerusalem had become a centre of hypocrisy and the courts of the Temple a place for trading. We need to think of our attitude to reverence in Church when we attend. Our Lord was furious at what went on and we know what He did about it.

Prayer:

> *"Teach us Lord to live by the Spirit"*

Wednesday in the fourth week of Lent

Quote:
"Behold, he that keepeth Israel: shall neither slumber nor sleep"
(Psalm 121 v4)

When Jesus went to Jerusalem for the last time, He was
going to the end of His own personal journey. He would
have turned a corner round a hill and seen in front of
Him the hill on which Jerusalem stands. He wept, for
the Jews were the people whom God had called to be a
kind of priesthood. But what did Our Lord see? It was
as though the word "failure" was written across the city.
Soon the tramp of Roman soldiers would be heard as
one of the most terrifying sieges in all history took place.
For a long time God had been building the city, in order
to make it truly His own. As we think of this scene, so
we pray for the Jewish Nation and her place in the
Middle East.

Prayer:
"Lord we pray that we may not fail you in the time of trial"

Thursday in the fourth week of Lent

Quote:

"This day is holy unto our Lord"
(Nehemiah 8 v10)

In that glance at the city which Jesus made, there is also the story of all our hearts. The way we recognise the presence of wrong in ourselves as we are doing this Lent, is instinctively to defend ourselves against God's approach. God is laying siege to us in a sense and what we call a conversion is when part of the defences falls. Pray that this comparison of ourselves to a city besieged by God may help us this Lent as we examine ourselves.

Prayer:
"We pray for greater faith as we look at ourselves today"

Friday in the fourth week of Lent

Quote:
*"The priests and Levites purified themselves and purified
the people and the gates and the wall"
(Nehemiah 12 v30)*

As we progress through Lent, we find sometimes that
the excuses we put up against God seem to be
outflanked. Our hearts seem changed in our attitude to
Him and to our brethren. Then we realise that change
continues almost as a miracle. This can meet with
unbelief and Lent is a good time to meditate on our
own personal conversion. We are almost with Jesus on
a corner tower of Jerusalem in the full knowledge that
God is all around us and yet we so often keep Him out.

Prayer:
"Lord may we have life through Your death"

Saturday in the fourth week of Lent

Quote:

*"Yea, rather, blessed are they that hear the
word of God and keep it"
(Luke 11 v28)*

Very often the barriers that we know so well that we
put up against God are a prejudice against some
teaching we hear or some liturgical practice. We make
a great song and dance perhaps about shaking our
neighbour's hand in Church, when we would think
nothing of doing so outside or even going further as is
done on the continent of giving him or her a kiss and a
hug as with the greeting of Orthodox Bishops and their
beards! Children draw pictures of God, usually an old
man with a long beard, but one child in a Liverpool
Cathedral exhibition some years ago had drawn a very
sad face streaming with tears — a six-year-old had
reached the heart of the matter. We do well to think on
his view of God, weeping at what we have done to His
world and His creation.

Prayer:

*"We pray that we may be able to accept those
with different views to our own"*

Fourth Sunday of Lent

Quote:
"Whence shall we buy bread that these may eat?"
(John 6 v5)

Lent is long — six weeks, so mediaeval man welcomed a rest from the rigours of his fast. Hence today, Refreshment Sunday, Laetare Sunday, Mothering Sunday — whatever name you call it by. Apprentices took a break from work and went home with gifts and girls brought flowers, the origins of our posies in Church. It is a time for rejoicing for the spring flowers are out. The Americans too keep a day in May when they celebrate Mother's Day, nothing to do with our mid-Lent Sunday. The custom was to go to the mother Church either of the Parish or to the Cathedral if possible as the mother of the Diocese. We honour our mothers, whether with us here or not and they in their turn when their children arrived home, made a special lunch with the Simnel cake.

Prayer:
"Help us, O Lord, to care for the common good of all,
as you went about doing good"

Monday in the fifth week of Lent

Quote:
"This is of a truth that prophet that should come into the world"
(John 6 v14)

We must think again about ourselves and Lent as the season is moving rapidly towards the Great fortnight. Our temptations are completely understood by Our Lord with all His sureness and the sympathy of His own human experience. This is what the world finds so difficult to understand when tragedy hits — that He is there not so we avoid it, but so that we can with His help bear it. We can't understand His temptations — we have already looked at that side of His ministry. In the wilderness truth met untruth — all choices were offered by the Devil but the one divine one was made. We are taught to pray that we avoid temptation and it is in the silence of prayer that we try to lead our lives.

Prayer:
"O Lord be at our side as we pray our way through Lent"

Tuesday in the fifth week of Lent

Quote:
"O Lord how amiable are thy dwellings, thou Lord of hosts"
(Psalm 84 v1)

Lent is a time for us to think about our Church, not so much the building, though that of course must be kept in good order as a sign of respect to our God, but the movement we belong to and have since our baptisms. There are times when we can be depressed at how we think the future may be going, especially when the media tells us congregations are declining. We should never believe all we read, because we know that 430 new Churches have been opened in the last twenty-five years, but attendances do vary. Perhaps we should be asking ourselves what we can do about the situation today.

Prayer:
"We pray that many will come to know you"

Wednesday in the fifth week of Lent

Quote:

*"My soul hath a desire and longing to enter
into the courts of the Lord"
(Psalm 84 v2)*

Following on from yesterday I found the following. In 1745 a certain Bishop Butler was asked to become Archbishop of Canterbury. He declared, "It is too late to try and support a failing Church" and declined the appointment. In a sense the Church has always been declining, even Our Lord lost one of His original choices, but polls suggest that we are still a God-believing Nation. We must be thankful for that and be revived this Lent for the work ahead.

Prayer:

*"We pray today for those of little faith,
that they may be strengthened"*

Thursday in the fifth week of Lent

Quote:

"Come and I will make you fishers of men"
(Matthew 4 v19)

Religion is here to stay. Millions believe. This gives meaning and purpose to our lives through these weeks leading to Easter. We have brief thoughts about our personal condition. Lent is a solemn time, but we no longer think of it in a Puritanical sense. Earlier times didn't. We still talk about "Friday fish". This is a survival and rather suggests a happy occasion as there is so much choice. Mind you, you must like fish! What we have to remember is not what we are actually doing about Lent, but the ultimate end of the time when the days have lengthened to Easter, and Easter itself is passed.

Prayer:

"We pray that we may work with others for the
furtherance of our congregations"

Friday in the fifth week of Lent

Quote:
"In every place your faith to God-ward is gone forth"
(1 Thessalonians 1 v8)

St Matthew wrote his Gospel somewhere towards the end of the first century, during a time of great persecution of the Church. There may come a time when followers of Christ can save their lives by abandoning their faith, but if they do, so far from saving them, they may be losing as they compromise themselves. In our own days it is not so much persecution as indifference and in many cases lack of education. We have time to meditate on what should be done to revive the faith.

Prayer:
"We pray, O Lord, for our friends and neighbours who say they are Christian in name but do not practise"

Saturday in the fifth week of Lent

Quote:

> *"I believed and therefore have I spoken"*
> *(Psalm 116 v10)*

Honesty is one of the great qualities. Our Lord shows it in His approach to us. No one can ever say that they have followed Jesus under false pretences. We are never bribed by the praise of an easy way. He doesn't offer peace, but glory. Our Lord challenges us but never asks us to face anything which He was not prepared to face Himself.

Prayer:

> *"Lord hear our prayer for all people. May they want to meet you in their daily lives"*

Passion Sunday

Quote:
"Verily, verily I say unto you before Abraham was, I am"
(John 8 v58)

Two weeks to go. Today we begin the annual commemoration of the last two weeks of Our Lord's earthly life and all that implies for us. Ultimately for us the cross must mean one of two things, everything or nothing in our lives. We have to accept Good Friday thankfully as the grounds for our salvation or completely reject it as unnecessary. I hope we shall see more of this as the week progresses. Stones were thrown at Jesus in today's Prayer Book Gospel reading. Read it to see why.

Prayer:
"Lord, we ask you to build a new spirit within us"

Monday in Passion Week

Quote:
"The Son of God who loved me and gave himself for me"
(Galatians 2 v20)

St Paul could never get over the fact that Jesus had died for him and again and again comes back to this point in his writings. Others much better qualified than I am have said that the little word "Me" in today's quote is the one to meditate on. For Paul there was complete reliance on Our Lord's Passion, none on his own efforts, considerable though they were by human standards.

Prayer:
"We pray in St Paul's steps that we may
place all our reliance on God"

Tuesday in Passion Week

Quote:

"The Lord is King for ever and ever"
(Psalm 10 v16)

To understand the background to these two weeks which lead to Easter Day, we must read our Bibles. A recent Archbishop is on record as writing, that the Old Testament is like a musical symphony on a grand scale. The theme, the melody, the tune is simple. It is what the composer does with it and how he expresses it that shows his skill. The basic theme of the Old Testament is "The Lord is King". The remainder of the books are how the Jews, a very literate race, interpreted the theme.

Prayer:

"O Lord we pray that we may read our
Bibles with understanding"

Wednesday in Passion Week

Quote:

"Behold the handmaid of the Lord"
(Luke 1 v38)

Jewish ideas about God and the theme of the Old Testament which we were looking at yesterday evolved over the ages. These ideas changed and lead to God choosing a Jewish girl, Mary as the Mother of His Son. With a theme like "God is King", can we really say that the Bible is irrelevant as so many seem to do nowadays?

Prayer:
"Lord we pray we may be as receptive as Mary was when the Angel Gabriel visited her"

Thursday in Passion Week

Quote:

> *"Teach me thy way, O Lord"*
> *(Psalm 86 v11)*

The theme "God is King" is a very good reason for looking at our Bibles, but there is a better reason for Christians, namely that Our Lord was and is a Jew. We sometimes forget that, perhaps because there are no contemporary pictures for us to look at. Jesus was bringing a new form of Judaism, a fulfilment of the old Jewish law not a destruction of it. "I came not to destroy but to fulfil", He says.

Prayer:

> *"We pray Lord that you will renew Your creation"*

Friday in Passion Week

Quote:

"Give ear unto my prayer and ponder the
voice of my humble desires"
(Psalm 86 v6)

The cross has to be central to our thinking. It has been since the Christian Church began. You see it everywhere and may even be wearing one. But what brought Jesus to Good Friday? The time He lived in was known for its worship of idols, immorality and slavery, but Our Lord speaks quite leniently about all three. His sternest words are for the insincere, the hypocrite, those who say one thing and do another. It was insincerity that brought Jesus to Good Friday.

Prayer:

"We pray that our every thought, word and deed
may be pleasing in Your sight"

Saturday in Passion Week

Quote:
"Be ye come out, as against a thief, with swords and staves?"
(Luke 22 v52)

To continue yesterday's ideas of insincerity which brought Jesus to His crucifixion, we must note that Caiaphas and the Sanhedrin tried to make out that Our Lord was put to death for inciting rebellion and that Judas played his part in this too. If, however, we read the accounts in the Gospels very carefully, a good lesson for this week, then we see that Jesus moved that last night in complete secrecy and with His customary reverence for the mystery of man's free will gave Judas the benefit of the doubt. Jesus went voluntarily and knew what He was doing.

Prayer:
"We pray that we may be delivered from all evils
and serve thee with a quiet mind"

Sunday next before Easter Sunday, Palm Sunday

Quote:
"Blessed be the King that cometh in the name of the Lord"
(Luke 19 v38)

Donkeys played an important part in Our Lord's earthly life. Before His birth a donkey carried His mother to the inn. After the birth a donkey carried Him into exile. Now on Palm Sunday a donkey bears Him in triumph into the capital city. The use of the donkey was to fulfil a prophecy in the Book of Zechariah. The crowds were enormous. No wonder the authorities met to discuss what to do about Jesus. Spare a thought for the donkey on that first Palm Sunday.

Prayer:
"Let us adore the Christ. Hosannah to the Son of David"

Monday in Holy Week

Quote:

"Who is this that cometh from Edom,
this that is glorious in his apparel?"
(Isaiah 63 v1)

The people who saw Jesus riding into Jerusalem yesterday would have been quite clear about the significance of the ride. They were being challenged as we are today. They cast Him out; do we do the same? No we in the words of the disciples say "The master has need of the donkey." Indeed He has need of us. All we have and are should be at His disposal.

Prayer:
"Heavenly Father walk with us today down every street and into every shop, that all may recognise who you really are"

Tuesday in Holy Week

Quote:

"I gave my back to the smiters and my cheeks
to them that plucked off the hair"
(Isaiah 50 v6)

Every ten years and occasionally in between, the villagers of Oberammergau, not far from Munich, produce a portrayal of the Passion and Death of Our Lord. This is to fulfil a vow made by their ancestors in 1633 during the plague. In the course of time visitors from all around come to see it and it is now a major production taking up a great deal of time. It was God's inscrutable decision as to when, where and how the redemption of mankind was to take place through Jesus, but this plan selected the place we call the Holy Land. The villagers fulfil their vow in a humble and dignified manner. Do we?

Prayer:

"Praise to Thee who for us on Calvary died"
(from 1970 text)

Wednesday in Holy Week

Quote:

"Christ was offered once to bear the sins of many"
(Hebrews 9 v28)

It was often Our Lord's custom to tell those He met and cured to remain silent and not to spread their news amongst their friends and relations, but Holy Week is different. It began in a great display of publicity. Jesus seems by nature to have been a humble retiring sort of person, but here is a blaze of glory. As the week passed so this glory faded and the people found their expectations of Him changing, bringing us to the quiet of the first part of Maundy Thursday evening.

Prayer:

"You have redeemed us by Your blood, O Lord"

Maundy Thursday

Quote:

"This do in remembrance of me"
(Luke 22 v19)

Every celebration of the Eucharist should be as it was for those first Apostles in the Upper Room — an hour or so of "Holy Communion" with God for this is the Lord's Supper. He is the host presiding over the feast. We are the guests.

Prayer:
"We pray that we may accept what we cannot understand"

Good Friday

Quote:

"Father, forgive them, for they know not what they do"
(Luke 23 v34)

Holy Saturday

Quote:
"When Joseph of Arimathea had taken the body,
he laid it in his own new tomb"
(Matthew 27 vv59-60)

Today we remember Our Lord's time in the sepulchre. In early times no services were held and the day was kept quietly. By tradition decorating of Churches for the following day took place in the afternoon. The Book of Common Prayer provides a Collect, Epistle and Gospel used at Ante-Communion without a celebration. One of the most important services of the Christian year takes place in the evening, the Paschal Vigil Service, the lighting of the new fire.

Prayer:
"We pray that Your Paschal Sacrifice, O Lord,
may draw all mankind to you"

Easter Day

Quote:

"For he is risen, as he said!"
(Matthew 28 v6)

St Joseph

March 19th

Quote:

"Joseph, her husband, being a just man"
(Matthew 1 v19)

There are not many references to Joseph in the New Testament. These few suggest a humble, kindly conscientious parent who followed Jewish tradition and apprenticed Jesus to the carpenter's bench. He is not mentioned again after the visit to the Temple when Our Lord was twelve. This has led to suggestions that he died and Our Lord was supporting a younger family. Certainly Jesus does not seem to have started His ministry until He was about thirty.

Prayer:
"We praise and thank you, O Lord, for placing Your Son under the watchful care of Joseph"

The Annunciation

Quote:
> *"Behold a virgin shall conceive and bear a son
> and shall call his name Immanuel"*
> *(Isaiah 7 v14)*

The events surrounding Jesus's birth bring special honour to women of all time. God could have chosen to appear in many forms, but instead chose to be incarnate of a young Jewish girl. Mary heads the list of many women mentioned in the Bible. She must have had very special qualities to be chosen and we honour her for them today.

Prayer:
> *"Hail Mary, full of grace, the Lord is with you.
> Alleluia, Alleluia"*